# Life
## is Hard Plays
# Rough

*Tales of Life, Loss and Love*

# TIM McCOOLE

*Life is Hard Plays Rough*
*Tales of Life, Loss and Love*


Copyright © 2021 by Tim McCoole.


Paperback ISBN:  978-1-63812-097-1
Hardcover ISBN:  978-1-63812-118-3
Ebook ISBN:  978-1-63812-098-8





Published by Green Sage Agency   08/13/2021


Green Sage Agency
1-888-366-9989
inquiry@greensageagency.com

# Contents

# Introduction

This manuscript is one of sadness yet one of celebration for though
there is sadness in loss there is celebration in a life reborn.

I have always believed in the healing power of the written
word thus the reason I wrote this book; to heal.

It has been said that no man is an island. No man can exist alone

" Life, loss and love " are words that play an immense role in ours but to which we
may pay little attention. Within the covers of this book, you will find how these
have steered the course of my life. I invite you to join me as we explore that path.

This book is fourteen years in the making but it could not have evolved without the
love, devotion and support of many, two of whom stand out from among the rest/

I met Martha Chavez in 1992 during Operation Restore Hope in Somalia
where. Simply by being the person that she is and her existence in my life at the
time, has become a dear lifelong friend. She was there to support me during
some very difficult periods in my life and has acted in the role of steadfast
supporter and critic whenever one of my writings made its way into her hands.
Without her there is sincere doubt that this manuscript would exist.

Keren came into my life through circumstances that can only be describes as Heaven
sent. Our paths crossed after the passing of my first wife Irene and I asked her to join her
life with mine shortly afterwards. It is to this chance meeting and lifelong commitment
that many of these verses owe their existence. I love you very much my angel

Tim

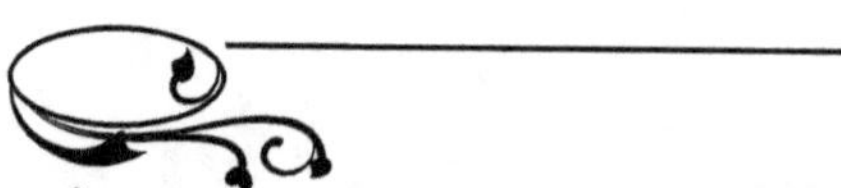

The verses found within this book are my own however in the time it took for this book to come to fruition, I happened upon other works that, at the time, I felt fit the mood of the book and I included them within these pages. I have delineated these works from my own by enclosing then in quotation marks and I ask that credit for them not be given to me. I would, however, like to extend my sincere thanks to those who's minds originated these words.

# Tears At A Stone

Tears, a silent testimony to love

Standing quietly at the stone

Looking down at your name

The name given you by the soul

Upon whom the stone now rests

A soul that is now free

Tears at a stone

A silent testimony to eternal love

# *In Memoriam*

"Healing' rain

Is coming down

It's coming closer to this old town"

It has been said that, when it rains

It is the angels crying

Crying over the loss of one of their children

Yet, rejoicing because another has been chosen to join their ranks

It rained the night she passed

The droplets falling from the eyes and the hearts of the angels

And the eyes and hearts of her loved ones

Who were standing there at her cold, sterile bedside

The room, itself, was cold and sterile

Yet there was a warmth

A warmth that radiated from the hearts of her children, her loved ones

Her nickname on the earth was Angel

Little did we know that it would become a prophecy

During the years of her illness I prayed

"Father. Please remove this illness from her and heal her"

He answered my prayer His way

He removed her from her illness

She has become her name and I am grateful

Life is hard

God is good

Let's dance

In the rain

# Thoughts From My Heart

A soft rain descends from the Heavens

Falling just hard enough to dapple the puddles

The iridescent leaves gently floating to the earth in concert with the raindrops

To join their brethren carpeting the soil below

The gentle breath of God

Creating music from the rustling leaves

Before those leaves are released from the bond

That has lovingly held them their entire life

To join their brethren in the great circle of life

The living waving as the fallen pass by

The majesty and eternal love of God

Is evident on this, my heaven on earth

From the moment I entered this, my own Garden of Eden

I was enveloped in love

A love that was made evident on that cold, grey October day

The day when my younger brother's soul was gently and lovingly released

And allowed union with the waters that he loved so much

The tears, that day, flowed like raindrops from the angels

Yet, with every tear, there came a release

Release from the pain of witnessing the destruction of a young life

Destroyed by drugs and alcohol

On that cold, gray October day, the angels, themselves, gave us their tears

As they welcomed another soul into their embrace

# Irene

I will never forget that day

The day that will, forever, live in infamy in my soul

The day you were taken from me, from our children

The tears of that day still come, and the grief overwhelms me

On the anniversary of your passing

It has been said that time is a great healer

A lifetime, itself, is not enough time to heal this grievous wound inflicted by your passing

But you are with me, still

In that warm hearth in my heart

A place where love and memories reside

It is never dark as your light reaches into all dark corners

I know that day will come where our hands will, once again join

Where my heart can relinquish this saddness it feels

But until that day comes, know this

Although you physically left me on that cold November night

You will remain with me

Deep in my heart

# Words

What are words? Are they a mere joining of letters

From an alphabet given us by the ages.

Do words have a meaning or are they merely sounds that are made?

Tell me this. How can the mere joining of these letters and sounds

Elicit human reactions of joy? Of pain

Are there words for every conceivable occasion

If so, what does one say to a child

Whose father is never coming back.

A dad who dies at the hands of an unseen foe.

The folded flag in his tiny hands all that is left

Memories in his heart all he has left to hug

A picture on the mantle all he has to fuel those memories

What does one say to a young woman

Who has chosen you as the one to give her heart, her hopes, her dreams, her life to?

Someone who, up to that time, was a relative unknown in her world

What do you say when you look into the loving eyes of a small child

And realize that life is truly a miracle and that this child is a blessing?

What words are used?

Are there any?

# Our Father / My Dad

"Our Father who art in Heaven"

It has been said that any man could be a father

But it takes someone with a little something special to be a daddy

Does this mean that He who conceived all, created all and sees all

Doesn't have what it takes to be a daddy just because he is called Father?

Somehow I don't think so as I, for one, still call Him daddy

Yes, I agree He is my Father but there is something special

I know that, just like my earthbound daddy, my picture rests on His mantlepiece

Alongside all of the others who call Him daddy

"Jesus loves me, this I know

For the Bible tells me so"

It is not the written word in the Bible that assures me

But Jesus, himself, by His words and His gifts given, without reservation

Yes, I agree, any man can be a father

I consider myself lucky

I have a Daddy

# Peace

The alarm pierces the early Sunday calm

My arm slithers from beneath the covers to silence this little electronic pest

And allow me a few more moments of repose in the land of dreams

My minds' eye, now awakened, envisions my favorite chair in the corner

A hot cup of my favorite coffee and my puppies for companionship

I laboriously slither from beneath my warmth much like a butterfly emerges from

Its cocoon

To begin a new day - a new life

Each sunrise is my opportunity for a new life

My chance to begin again

Coffee in hand, puppies waiting patiently for the love I have to give them

I sit in the familiar, welcoming cushions of my chair

It is almost as though they are saying, "come to me. I bring peace.

Come to me Tim. On me you will find rest from your labors and peace

For your soul

I feel that peace as I sit, my left hand reaching over to scratch the ears of my

Puppy Mocha

Within that peace I find myself speaking with Him who created me

And Him with me.

I find myself praying, thanking Him for all that was before and all that

Is to come

It is in this prayer that I ,cannot help but, wonder

Are these words my own

Or are they part of an eternal script ascribed from the quills of angels
He who created all, knows all and sees all knows these words as they are
Part of the script
He knows my needs before I am aware of this knowledge
When I sit, coffee in hand, with my puppies, in the early morning silence
Should the words be difficult for my tongue to form
All my soul needs do is read the script
And leave the rest to Him

# Piget

She's a piget

Not even large enough to be called a piglet

She is a lillipution brindle and white puppy

A bundle of energy that wandered into my home

From the city streets

Crystal blue eyes capable of piercing through to your very soul

A little round tummy

Giving her the persona of a tiny, four-legged Saint Nick

Come to bestow love and blessings to all whose path she crosses

Dimunitive little paws in constant synchronized motion

Searching, exploring this strange new world into which she has been welcomed

Tiny little pink tongue giving prayerful thanks to every cheek she encounters

The Lord works in mysterious ways

He sees a need and fulfills a need

When I heard of her from my daughter, I prayed

"Father, please guide me and allow me to do what is best

I truly have no room as there are five dogs here now.

I have no room except in my heart"

Into my heart she crawled

I made room in my home

# Question For You

Tell me this

What is wrong with me?

What is wrong with my eyes?

They refuse to see the beauty that envelops me every moment of every  day

Oh, they see the outside beauty

The full moon on a chilly spring morning

The love and loyalty of my puppies

But there is something missing

What? What could be missing?

Here I am, a man who has been blessed in many ways, to many to count

Blessings that, in my eyes, are undeserved

Blessings given me as gifts

Gifts for a good deed done and long forgotten

What am I missing?

My eyes look into the trusting eyes of my puppy and allow me to feel her love

Yet they miss the loving eyes that follow me every moment of every day

The eyes of my children, of my daughter, my grandson, my spouse

Gifts given to me but unseen by me

Selective sight brought on by anger and frustration blind me to what I should see

My beautiful young wife, a true angel

Given to me as a gift to fill the void left by the passing of one before

My eldest daughter, given me by that one before

Flawed in many ways but still a diamond that I would give all my worldly possessions to retain

My grandson, a child wise beyond his years, a man in child's garb

Given to me as a second chance to correct all that I did or did not do as a father of my own

My eldest son, my youngest son

Both grown into me that any father would sell his very soul to call them his own

My pride knows no bounds as I am able to call them my own

My youngest daughter

From the moment of her birth I know this child was both a gift and gifted

A young lady who's love and beauty is as rare as a violet rose

Holy Father I ask you, please, to give me your eyes for just one second

Give me your eyes so I can see

Everything that I've been missing

I have, but one life on this Earth

Allow me, please, to see

# Soldier

I met a soldier today

No, I did not shake their hand and say thank you for all you do

Nor did I meet their gaze from across the room

Or pay for a meal that they consumed

But I did meet them

My grandson and I were in a park on a major military airbase

When a large, gray aircraft descended from the sky

And settled upon the earth as softly and gently

As an autumn leaf kissing the tall grass

As though the pilot did not wish to wake those sleeping inside

As it rolled slowly to a stop, it was met

A young woman, clothed in black, face wet with tears

A young boy, much like the one by my side, clutching her hand

Eyes wide, wondering

Six smartly uniformed brethren of the one who slept inside

A long, black car, doors open, waiting to receive

The six brought forth, from the aircraft, an American flag

Beneath that flag lie this young woman's memories

Her mother. Her father, her sister, her brother, her son, her daughter

Her soulmate

I found my old bones stiffening into the long unused, almost forgotten position of
Attention

The arthritic fingers of my right hand straightening

The hand, on its own volition, rising to meet my forehead

Saluting one unknown to me, yet known to me

Rendering honors to one who gave all

Yes, today I met a soldier

# A Letter To Keren

Are you real or are you the most beautiful dream I have ever had?

Are you an angel or a figment of my imagination?

Are you someone my mind fabricated to fill the void, to soothe the pain?

You made me laugh when I felt like crying

You took me dancing when I couldn't take a step

You helped me set goals when I was dying

You brought me wildflowers and suddenly I had roses

You showed me dewdrops and suddenly I had diamonds

You sang to me and I heard angelic choirs

You placed a ring on my finger and I found a home

You hold my hand and my heart and, in you I found a home

On that March day, when our hands touched,

the sky became a little bluer, the birds sang a little sweeter

When you said "I do" these words rang like cathedral bells in my soul

# Autograph

Please, if you will, tell me this

What is an autograph?

No, I don't mean the name of some celebrity

Scrawled on any material available

No, I mean the type of autograph

That tells the world around you what you've done

What you have accomplished in your time on Earth,

Where you have been

Your legacy, in other words

What will my legacy be? I wish I could tell you

I do know that I was placed here for a purpose

I was given a gift to use as I choose

I'm given that gift anew every morning my eyes are allowed to open

A gift of a new day, another chance

This morning I was honored to view another mans' legacy

Before me, in the early spring sky was a full, ivory moon

Veiled in wispy flowing clouds

Like the veil of a new bride on the happiest day of her life

This evening I bore witness to, yet another gift

Those same gossamer clouds enveloping a setting sun

In such a way so as to light entire sky ablaze with fiery reds and oranges and iridescent
yellows

The likes of which go unseen by those who choose not to see

Those blind to the gifts offered

One of the gifts that I have been given are eyes that see

I chooses to use that gift wisely

# Heaven

I held Heaven in my arms today

It was, but a small piece, about seven pounds

Swaddled in a soft, blue blanket

A small piece of heaven given to me by my youngest child

Small, pudgy hands with fingers in perpetual motion

Grasping my own as if to say

"Hi Poppi. I'm happy to meet you"

Little crystal blue orbs gazing deeply into my own

Puffy little lips in constant motion as if to say

"What are you waiting for? I'm hungry!"

My life is now complete for I held a small piece of Heaven in my arms today

# How To Make A Puppy

1.  Take a clean dustmop, although it need not be completely clean
2.  Add four short legs to the underside of the mop
3.  Attach a small, round head with two marble – like eyes that pierce your very soul
4.  Give it a short tail preferably with a crook on the end of it
5.  Instill in it a personality somewhere between sweet and totally psychotic

There you have it, my puppy Mocha

From the first day I met, a bond was formed, a bond that grows stronger with each passing day. She, at one time, belonged to another who cared not for her, neglecting her to the point of endangering her health, breaking her spirit and seriously diminishing her will to live.

She is now mine as I took her from that environment and through love and time, repaired some of the damage afflicted. Although there may be some residual remaining, this little girl now knows the meaning of love.

# I Wonder

What is love?

I mean what is the definition of love?

Although the official Websters Dictionary definition eludes, I do have a few ideas

Love is that feeling that enveloped me when our hands first touched

That first hug was more than my arms holding you

It was a bonding of our hearts

A bond that grows stronger with each passing moment

Love equates to beauty

Beauty is what I see every morning when I gaze into your sleepy eyes

Eyes that brighten with the morning tea

Love is that feeling I experience when I look into those eyes

Keren. You are the reason for my awakening every morning

I know that I have said this before, almost to the point of my words seeming empty but

I promise you, it is not my lips speaking them. It is my soul

Please believe me when I say that I love you. More than today. Not as much as tomorrow

# My Today

My eyes look to the front of me

To the future

My eyes don't look behind me

To the past; to what once was

The past has been filled with memories

Some beautiful, some painful

All there in the annals of my life, each moment a page turned

The future waits, patiently, for its turn

Its turn to be filled with memories

Memories of my young spouse

As beautiful today as the day she joined her life to mine

An undeserved gift

Memories of a man-child e are raising together

A second chance

Memories of, holding in my arms, a piece of Heaven, given me by my youngest

I have lived my life, yet my life is yet to be lived

I await each sunrise

Anxious to welcome the future

# Directions

"Red sky at night
Sailors delight"

This short. descriptive sailors' ditty is continually with me as my nightly sojourn home allows me a vision of the fiery heavens. As I gaze upon this wonder of God given beauty, a feeling of peace with the warmth and tenderness of a mother's hug envelops me and I cannot help but feel blessed.

As I scribe these words one of my blessings cuddles up next to me. The closeness of our bodies her guarantee that she will never lose my love. Her body next to mine her guarantee I will never lose hers. Her small, crystal blue love filled eyes say "thank you. Thank you for taking me and loving me when here was no other."

My pen moves in its own while my soul revels in the silence surrounding me. It is in this veil of silence that my other blessing reveals themselves to me. My young angel, given me to heal a shattered heart, playing with her puppy Precious in the bedroom. My grandson, given as a second chance leafing through a firefighter book and pointing out, in great detail, all the trucks to me.

All of this was given freely to me not because I earned it or deserved any of it but because I am a child of the Father who gives freely to all who believe.

# The Voice Of God

Silence

The absence of sound

Or is it?

It has been said that, in the silence if you choose to listen you can

Hear God speaking to you

As I sit in quiet repose and listen to the silence

I hear His voice

It is not the voice of human but of His creations

The songs of the spring birds

The soft breeze, like the breath of God, rustling the leaves

Tell me, is silence truly the absence of sound

Or is it we simply choose not to listen?

# Sounds Of Silence

Stepping from my home into the early morning calm

I find that I must stop

Stop and listen

Listen to the sounds of silence

That golden time when the world finds a moment of calm and peace reigns supreme

My eyes are drawn upward to the azure sky

The full moon flirting behind gossamer clouds

Like a bashful, little girl hiding behind her veil

As I gaze upon this wonderous site, my minds eye cannot help, but envision

Dad, Irene, Danny, Uncle Mike, Gram, Nana, Aunt Louise, Pepe', Uncle John

Looking down on me

Wishing they could be with me and I with them

My feet refuse to move until I pay those who have gone before homage

I find an inner piece as I say good morning to Irene, Dad, Danny and all the others

Who find their home with Jesus

They are now at peace

A peace I find in the early morning silence

# How

I am far from those who gave me birth

Far from the soil that felt my childhood feet

Distanced from those who shared their early years with me

You are not of distant birth

This is your soil, the soil of your birth

Could it, possibly, be that I was placed here so that our lives could be joined?

Could it, possibly, be that your life was as it was so your heart could meet mine?

I'm sorry, but the answer is not mine to give

I can only gaze into your eyes and be thankful

The answer may not be mine to have but I am thankful that your heart is

# Two Rings

I wear two rings, one on each hand

So what, I hear you say

There are many among us who do the same

Possibly not, I counter, for the reason I do

You see, the ring on my lest hand, an ornately carved of white gold from the Emerald isle

Was given to me by a woman whose dream I made come true

A dream of finding a man to care for he, someone to fulfill a lifelong wish for children, a lifelong wish for love

A woman sent to me to fill a void left by the passing of one before, one who once held my heart

One who still shares my heart

Hence the ring on the right hand

A simpler band of gold showing all that, although she is no longer with me physically

Although I hold another in my arms

I hold both in my heart

# What Is A Friend

How does one define the term "friend"? If I were to follow the teachings of Mr. Webster, a friend would be; 1. A person who knows and likes another or 2; A person who favors and supports.

May I, please, take this a step further?

A friend is one, who, after a brief encounter, chooses to remain. A friend is one who steps into a life with no direction and gives it direction. One who greets you with a smile no matter what their day held for them. A friend is one who takes precious time from their own life to hold you up when your world has come to an end. A friend is that light in the darkness.

I wrote a letter in the sand and it was answered………by you. You are a gift for a good deed done long ago and long forgotten. I will cherish that gift today, tomorrow and for all the tomorrows I am given. Take my heart. It is yours.

# Wonder

Keren, I have often wondered. Where would my life be if I didn't have you in it? I have often gazed upon your sleeping form wrapped in a cocoon of blankets as though the sunrise would bring about a morphing from the blanket form into the angel that blesses my life.

I have heard it said that God works in mysterious ways and does all according to a master plan. Could that miniscule spark we felt with that first embrace His way of saying we belonged together? If do, then I feel truly blessed as I am not deserving of such a gift as you.

I ask you, please, to believe me when I say I love you, it is not my lips that ae saying them. It's my heart.

# Vows

We have traveled a long, broken road to get where we are today

Today I choose you to be my wife, my soulmate

As I stand here and look at you, I see all that I fell in love with

Today I gladly take on the responsibility of caring for my partner, comforting my love and laughing with my best friend

I promise to protect you life with mine. I promise not to go down old roads with you but to create new paths for us to explore together.

I promise to love you more with each passing day

We have shared much to get here but the best is yet to come

Today I gladly give to you my hand to hold, my life to share, my heart to keep

From this day forward you will not walk alone

My heart will be your shelter, my arms your home

Lastly, I give to you one dozen long stemmed red roses. Eleven of them are real. One is not. Keren, you will have all of my love until that last one dies

Tim McCoole, (known as Poppi to his children and grandchildren) is a twice retired, military an civil service father of four, grandfather of six. He makes his home with his wife Keren, grandson Matt, and daughter Ryan in San Antonio, Texas. This book is his first publication and, although fourteen years in the making, is a compilation of his thoughts and feeling over those years